THE THEORY OF
RENÉ GIRARD

A VERY SIMPLE INTRODUCTION

WRITTEN AND ILLUSTRATED BY
CARLY OSBORN

AGS

This book is dedicated to my daughter Ella;
and to the memory of the luminous René Girard.

ISBN: 978-1542352314

Second Edition Reprint, 2017
First and Second Editions, 2016
3 4 5 6   19 18 17

Published by the Australian Girard Seminar
www.australiangirardseminar.org

CONTENTS

INTRODUCTION

This book is a very simple introduction to the theory of René Girard. His theory covers the origins of desire, the causes of human conflict, the development of Western culture, and, ultimately, the escalation of violence.

I wrote it because I wanted a little book I could leave on my coffee table that my friends could pick up, flick through, and get a basic idea of what Girardian theory is about.

A book of this nature necessarily reduces some fairly complex ideas to their simplest form. The resulting gaps and weaknesses are the fault of my book, not Girard's theory. If either the theory or the gaps pique your interest, I encourage you to read further, and discover the rich, complex and thought-provoking ideas in the theory of René Girard.

1.

MIMETIC DESIRE

The cornerstone of Girard's theory is the idea of 'mimetic desire'. 'Mimetic' comes from the Greek word 'mimesis', which means to imitate.

The idea of 'mimetic desire' is that our desires do not happen spontaneously from inside us, but instead, we imitate the desires of others.

Let's call these two guys A and B.

We call A the 'subject'—our main character. B is what Girard calls A's 'model'. A admires B. He wants to be like B. He observes B, and he learns what to desire from B. If B desires it, it becomes desirable in A's eyes.

One way to represent this is with a triangular diagram.

A thinks that his desire for the hat is a straight line between them. But really, he gets to the hat via B. Sometimes Girard calls this 'triangular desire' instead of 'mimetic desire'.

We've all seen mimetic desire in action. A child wants a toy because his sister is playing with it. Once she drops it, he doesn't want it any more.

Advertisers use mimetic desire all the time. *See, George Clooney desires this watch! Beyonce wears this perfume!* Our desire is provoked in response to seeing our models desire those objects. We want what they want. This is mimetic desire.

Girard's first book laid out his theory of mimetic desire. It's called *Deceit, Desire & the Novel*. In it, Girard argues that 'great novelists' understand that desire is mimetic. Bad novels, he says, repeat the 'lie' that our desires are spontaneous, but truly 'great novels' reveal the truth.

He starts with the example of *Don Quixote*, a famous Spanish novel. If you're not familiar with the story, Don Quixote is a guy who decides he wants to be a knight, like in medieval times.

It all starts because Don Quixote reads a book about Amadeus of Gaul, a famous knight. Don Quixote devotes his life to imitating Amadeus, and his fantasy consumes him. He gets a horse and a suit of armour and gallops about the countryside pretending that windmills are enemy knights.

Girard is saying, "Look! The story of Don Quixote shows the truth that the protagonist is imitating the desires of his model."

Next, Girard takes us one step further.

When B sees A desiring the hat, the hat becomes even more desirable to B. A's desire provokes B's desire. They're equally copying each other, provoking more and more imitative desire.

A and B might be friends. But their desire for the hat will get in the way: they will start to see each other as rivals. It could get ugly.

How ugly could it get? Well, that depends.

If B is a fictional character in a movie, like Batman, then A can't really hate him because he doesn't exist.

If B is A's favourite football celebrity, then A might be a bit jealous, but probably won't see B as his immediate rival; instead, A feels that B is far above him, in a world that's out of reach. B will never know about it.

If A and B are next-door-neighbours, then trouble is brewing.

This is what Girard calls the 'height of the triangle'.

The further away from each other A and B are, the less likely they are to see each other as rivals, and end up jealous and resentful of each other.

If they are within reach of each other, living in the same social world, Girard calls this 'internal mediation'.

next-door neighbours

If they're in separate worlds, this is 'external mediation'.

External mediation is pretty safe. A admires Batman. He wants the things that Batman wants, but never thinks of Batman as a rival. It works fine.

Internal mediation, however, is big trouble. Why? Read on.

2.

MIMETIC CRISIS

A and B see each other as rivals. The bonds and niceties that hold society together will strain under the pressure. Rivalry leads to resentment, and eventually to violence.

Each person wants to eliminate his or her rivals. Violence is met with retaliation: more violence.

This is a big problem, because happy, healthy communities need their members to feel allied with one another.

Neighbours are there to help each other. We're on the same team. We're better together.

But mimetic desire leads to rivalry, which leads to what Girard calls 'mimetic crisis', which looks like this:

Mimetic crisis is the state in which communal bonds have broken down. Everyone has turned upon everyone else.

The mimetic nature of human actions means that violent acts will just cause more violence.

The nature of violence is to escalate, and escalate…

How do we stop it before the little stick people all massacre each other??

Girard's next couple of books cover this problem: how do communities escape mimetic crisis?

3.
THE SCAPEGOAT

The answer may be familiar to anyone who has been in a kindergarten playground, corporate boardroom or a modern democracy: the members of the community gang up together against one unlucky victim, and blame him (or her) for the crisis.

They chase him away. They beat him with clubs. They hang him from a tree. They vote him out of the council. One way or another, the scapegoat takes the blame, and takes a violent punishment.

And incredibly, all the other members of the group—who *were* at each others' throats—now see each other as allies in the fight against the guilty victim.

Instead of Me against You, it's Us against The Enemy.

And so the community reconciles, and joins together again as one.

One love... one heart...

Of course, the crisis wasn't really the scapegoat's fault. But the members of the community believe that it was. They *have* to believe that it was—because their newfound peace is based on having gotten rid of that troublesome intruder.

Girard thinks that the Scapegoat Mechanism, as he calls it, began spontaneously at the dawn of humanity. Communities in crisis turned on scapegoats (often people who were already marginalised, like foreigners or those with physical deformities), expelled the scapegoat, reconciled, and lived to (literally) fight another day.

But over time, they started to notice that this was a handy way to fix a crisis. Got a problem? Find out whose fault it is, and shove them off a cliff!

4.
SCAPEGOAT RITUALS & MYTHS

Girard looks at a number of ancient rituals and notices a recurring theme: a victim is sacrificed to ensure the safety and health of the rest of the community. The victim is blamed not only for social problems, but for droughts, plagues, anything that disrupts the community.

The scapegoat takes the blame for everything, and getting rid of the scapegoat is the cure for everything.

These rituals, he says, are the basis of early religions. The scapegoat may be a poisonous intruder, but his death also saves and restores the community, so he is seen as a pretty potent force—eventually, as a god. This is a tricky concept, but it goes something like this:

Imagine A and B are standing in a field, chatting:

A: *Things have been great ever since we killed that weird old blind woman.*

B: *Yeah, she really polluted everything. The drought, the fighting, they all went away since we killed her.*

A: *Even that terrible rash I had. After she died it cleared right up!*

B: *She must have been very powerful to poison everything.*

A: *And powerful enough to fix everything too, and make it rain and stuff.*

B: *Wow. Do you reckon she was, like, a goddess?*

A: *Yeah, she must've been. Ordinary old women don't have super powers, dude.*

B: *We should build a shrine to her. She saved us.*

A: *She nearly killed us first, though. And she gave me a rash.*

B: *Gods are like that. Help me lift these big rocks.*

Girard says that ancient communities eventually ritualised their scapegoating. Why wait until things get really bad? Better to sacrifice someone regularly just to be on the safe side.

So an ancient community gets together at, say, harvest time. They have a feast, then drag some unfortunate partygoer (probably the guy with the bad eye, since he

seems to carry a curse) onto the altar. The priest chops off his head, and off goes the scapegoat, taking all the community's ills with him.

Everyone cheers and feels like things are going to be okay. Then they build a statue of bad-eyed Bob and worship it.

This simplifies into a few sentences what Girard explores for hundreds of pages. But the key point is that the scapegoat mechanism started as spontaneous acts but developed into formal rituals.

Alongside the rituals arise complex cultural rules that enforce the 'Us and Them' system: taboos about food, sex, status, all kinds of ways to know who is In and who is Out.

In between the sacrifices, the members of the community replay it over in their minds, by telling the story of what happened.

Remembering it lets them go through all the emotions of the ritual itself—the anxiety and unrest, the collective action against the scapegoat, the violence, the huge relief that things are okay again. The stories are almost as good as actually doing it. People enjoy telling the story to each other around the fireside. Girard sees these stories behind what we know as *myths*.

Myths are stories with religious or cultural importance, that are treasured and passed on in a community.

Myths, like all good tales, don't let the truth get in the way of a good story. So the story of 'how we chopped Bob's head off' becomes the myth of Bob the Mighty, who had ten heads and whose evil eye slew everyone he looked at, who died and whose body broke into thousands of raindrops that broke the drought and brought abundant crops to the land.

From the Aztec myth of Tecuciztecatl and Nanauatzin, to the Roman legend of Romulus and Remus, Girard sees myths as the Scapegoat Mechanism in story form. Telling the myth reinforces the community's identity: 'The scapegoat was guilty. We got rid of Them, and we are Us.'

Eventually, as communities become more 'civilised', they quit sacrificing people and just tell their scapegoat-myths in more elaborate ways…

5.
MYTH BECOMES TRAGEDY

As societies become more 'civilised', and move away from the whole sacrificing-people-on-the-altar thing, they put more effort into telling their myths. Because the community still needs the Scapegoat Mechanism as badly as ever. Rivalry and resentment still build up as a result of mimetic desire. A pressure-release-valve is essential.

Girard looks at Ancient Greece and their impressive theatre—especially their tragedies.

He notes that the plot of a tragedy is just like the sequence of the Scapegoat Mechanism: a community is doing okay until a sudden and terrible crisis; the tragic hero is revealed to be the cause of the crisis; the hero suffers terribly, is exiled or killed; and peace is restored, but at the hero's cost.

The story of Oedipus follows this pattern: he doesn't mean to do it, but he commits incest with his mother, which causes massive social and environmental crises.

He gouges out his own eyes and flees the city in order to save it.

Girard thinks that *Oedipus* is just another story in a long, long tradition of scapegoat-myths. That tradition is a big part of our cultural history. These recurring stories aren't just entertainment: they're a worldview passed down the generations. They reinforce that ancient, enduring belief that crises are caused by Them, outsiders who pollute Us. That the lone scapegoat is guilty, and the community is innocent.

But there was another tradition, with its own worldview and its own myths and stories, that impacted Western culture not long after the Ancient Greek era. And that's when things start getting really interesting.

6.

MYTHS THAT DON'T FIT

Girard was busily cataloguing the recurring pattern of the Scapegoat Mechanism in myths and religious texts, when he noticed something odd. The stories in the Old Testament of the Bible were different. Sure, they told stories of communities in crisis who turned on a victim, but they told the stories *from the victim's point of view*. In other words, they revealed that the victim was innocent, and the community just looking for a scapegoat.

Maybe this was because the Jews were often victims themselves. Girard thought there might be more to it— an exploration that lead him, eventually, to a religious conversion. But the key point is this: the stories of the

Old Testament did the one thing that a useful scapegoat-myth can never, ever do—blame the community and absolve the victim.

Like the story of Joseph and his resentful brothers, who kidnap him and sell him into slavery. The narrative takes the side of the victim, against his persecutors.

That's not a useful myth, in terms of the Scapegoat Mechanism. In fact, even hearing that story is pretty dangerous. It tells us the one thing that will really get in the way of our scapegoating habits: the Scapegoat Mechanism is always built on a lie. Girard calls these Bible stories 'anti-myths': they're the usual kind of myths, but told from the opposite side.

If this Jewish narrative tradition of anti-myths wasn't enough, says Girard, along comes someone whose actions will be a potent illustration of the perversity of the Scapegoat Mechanism. Jesus of Nazareth is executed by a malicious populace, and the subsequent narratives recording his execution become the core texts of a new religious culture—Christianity.

Girard sees the adoption of Christianity as a revolutionary shift in Western culture. Its texts, instead of affirming the Scapegoat Mechanism, denounce it. It shines light on the true causes of persecution and violence. It is, frankly, going to cause a lot of trouble.

7.

VIOLENCE & APOCALYPSE

The Scapegoat Mechanism needs to pull off a deceptive illusion: that the scapegoat is guilty. The influence of Christianity, says Girard, ruined the illusion.

Judeo-Christian Scripture tells the stories of many innocent scapegoats, and finally of Jesus of Nazareth who is not only innocent but who shows forgiveness instead of retaliating, breaking the cycle of escalating mimetic violence.

Our culture was radically affected by this religion that 'takes the side of the victims'. We have gradually, and

increasingly, become aware that not only Jesus of Nazareth but all victims of scapegoating are innocent.

Girard doesn't claim that Christianity and its Scriptures are the only source of insight about the Scapegoat Mechanism and its perversity. He sees 'anti-mythical' ideas in some Ancient Greek plays, for instance, and in a few non-Western sources (today's Girardian scholars are adding to this, looking at other texts and cultures).

But Girard's focus is on the history of Western culture. In this context, he says that Judeo-Christian Scripture did two important things:

1. It consistently takes that opposite point of view, declaring the innocence of the scapegoat, and

2. It was a major shaping force upon an entire society and culture, and so for generations, everyone was influenced by it.

The result is that we can no longer have really effective Scapegoat Mechanisms, in story form or in the real world of violence, exclusion and persecution.

You'd think that this awareness would be a good thing. But Girard says it is only good *if* we're willing to give up mimetic conflict, with its endlessly repeating violence. Willing to stop retaliating, not because the Scapegoat Mechanism rescues us, but just because we see what a mess we're making, and choose to be peaceful instead.

Unfortunately, we're not willing to do this. So what do we do?

It's not good news. Instead of stopping our scapegoating, we increase it. In Girard's words:

> 'This lack of efficiency often means that there are more rather than fewer victims. As in the case of drugs, consumers of sacrifice tend to increase the doses when the effect becomes more difficult to achieve.'

We're in denial. We don't want to admit that the scapegoat is innocent. So we desperately accuse and expel more and more and more victims.

Ironically, a lot of this violence has been and is done in the name of Christ. Girard thinks that turning Christianity into a reason for violence is stupid, yet predictable. Humans would rather keep scapegoating than admit that it's wrong.

Girard sees the escalation of violence in the apocalyptic vision of Christian Scripture—the apocalypse not as a Deity's wrath but as human violence retaliating back and forth, always escalating, until the whole world is a war zone. Scripture, according to Girard, describes a future in which humanity, rather than 'renouncing retaliation', instead chooses escalating violence.

Some Girardian scholars say that 'the apocalypse began at Verdun'. The 20th century certainly saw global violence on an unprecedented scale. In the 21st century, mimetic rivalry and conflict has everyone pushing and shoving for domination. Political violence takes many forms: the Western exploitation of the developing world, the increasing gap between rich and poor, terrorism and acts of ill-defined 'war'.

Girard says that the September 11th attacks in the USA caused a 'flash of awareness' that we are on a path of escalating violence that leads to apocalypse. However, he says a 'blanket of silence' quickly covered up this insight, and we went back to returning violence for violence.

8.

SO WHAT NEXT?

This is more or less where Girard's theory ends. Humanity, driven by mimetic desire and rivalry, aware that scapegoating is perverse, but in denial. Turning on more and more victims to try and get relief. Returning violence for violence. Cruising toward total apocalyptic war.

The example of the 'forgiving victim', personified for Girard by Christ, continues to invite us to live another way. To choose mercy instead of vengeance.

Girard sees hope in the possibility that we might realise what we're doing before it's too late.

Over 200 million people were killed by war and political violence in the 20th century.

I can't hear you. I'm under a blanket of silence.

FAQ

Q. What about my desire for a peanut butter sandwich right now? Is that mimetic desire?

Probably not. Girard distinguishes between desire and other kinds of 'wanting' like needs and appetites. If you're hungry, and you really like peanut butter, then it's probably not mimetic desire. You need food, and you feel like peanut butter instead of jam today. However, if you're at school and all the cool kids have been bringing peanut butter sandwiches for lunch—you get the idea.

Q. What if there are enough hats for everybody? Then A and B don't need to be rivals.

This is a very important point: *it's not really about the hat*. A admires B. He thinks B has really got that special something, something that makes B happy and complete. So A copies B—and gets the same hat (or house or car or haircut or whatever). But having the hat doesn't make A feel happy and complete. So he either ditches the hat and tries to copy B in some other way, or decides that B wasn't really cool anyway—ditching B for another model who he hopes really does have the secret to happiness.

The point, as you can see, is that A will never be satisfied. Because what he's really chasing isn't the material objects—it's about the fantasy of coolness and completeness, the dream of being somebody different, somebody better. But B doesn't really have the secret to happiness; in fact, B is busy admiring and copying his own models, haunted by *his* sense of being incomplete.

Sure, a shortage of hats won't help the situation. But an abundance of hats won't fix it, either. Give A a hat, and he'll rejoice for a second, then realise it doesn't do the trick, and throw it aside. He'll keep believing that completeness is out there, that his models have acquired it, and that his rivals are in his way.

Q. So is all mimetic desire bad?

No. Girard says that we're imitative by nature, and that this can lead to good things too. A child develops by copying those around her. I admire my friend's ability on the piano, and so I learn to play. But positive imitation can turn into resentful rivalry in a flash: I'm going to become a great pianist, and then everyone will applaud for *me*.

How to avoid destructive mimetic desire, and make it a force for good, is one of the themes of Girard's later work—and an issue that has been taken up by the next generation of Girardian thinkers: psychologists, sociologists, theologians and others.

Q. Is mimetic theory supposed to explain everything?

No. Mimetic theory states that humans are imitative, and that this causes rivalry and violence. A lot of things result from this, and can be explained with mimetic theory. But it doesn't explain everything in the universe.

A good analogy is the principle of gravity. Gravity explains some things, like why an apple drops to the ground. Gravity doesn't explain why wood is flammable. Gravity is there while the fire is burning, keeping the logs from rising up into the air, but it is not the reason why wood burns. In the same way, mimesis is always around us, but it doesn't explain every phenomenon.

Q. Is Girardian theory only about Western culture?

No. Girard's work on ritual and myth looks at lots of different cultures, though his later work focuses on Christianity and the West. He believed that mimesis was part of human nature, and that every culture has developed rituals and institutions to try and manage mimetic crisis and violence. Non-Western scholars, including Muslim, Buddhist and other thinkers, are now applying Girardian theory to studies of their own cultures and religions, finding sources of insight about scapegoating in their texts and traditions.

RECOMMENDED READING

If you can, start with *The Girard Reader* (1996), edited by James G. Williams. It's a great collection of selected chapters of Girard's most important books, with introductions explaining each one.

SELECTED BOOKS BY GIRARD

Deceit, Desire and the Novel: Self and Other in Literary Structure (1966)

Violence and the Sacred (1977)

The Scapegoat (1986)

I See Satan Fall Like Lightning (2001)

Battling to the End (2009)

BOOKS EXPLAINING GIRARDIAN THEORY

Discovering Girard by Michael Kirwan

René Girard: Violence and Mimesis by Chris Fleming

René Girard's Mimetic Theory by Wolfgang Palaver

BOOKS USING GIRARDIAN THEORY

There are many of these, notably two excellent series: *Studies in Violence, Mimesis, & Culture* by MSU Press, and *Violence, Desire, and the Sacred*, published by Continuum.

There are also lots of articles using mimetic theory in the academic journal *Contagion*, which is devoted to Girardian scholarship and comes out annually.

FIND OUT MORE

The international society of scholars of Girard's theory is called The Colloquium on Violence and Religion (COV&R). They have an annual conference, and publish the journal *Contagion*. Their website also lists local Girardian organisations in various countries around the world.

You can become a member of COV&R and get book subscriptions, journal access and other cool stuff.

www.violenceandreligion.com

Imitatio is the international body which supports research, education, and publications building on René Girard's mimetic theory.

www.imitatio.org

RENÉ GIRARD
1923–2015

René Girard was one of the 20th century's most significant theorists. He was a philosopher of social science, a historian and literary critic, whose work has influenced the disciplines of literary criticism, political theory, anthropology, theology, psychology, sociology, economics, cultural studies, and philosophy.

He was born in Avignon, France, in 1923. He moved to the USA in 1947 and spent most of his academic career there, though he continued to write his works primarily in French. He held a number of distinguished positions at American universities, and was inducted into the prestigious Académie Française as one of their *immortels:* they described him as 'the new Darwin of the human sciences'.

He died on Nov. 4, 2015.

ABOUT THE AUTHOR

Dr Carly Osborn is a Postdoctoral Research Fellow at the University of Adelaide, within the Australian Research Council Centre of Excellence for the History of Emotions. Her PhD was a study of modern tragedies and Girardian theory, and she now researches and teaches on the topic of ritual spectacles of violence.

She has received a number of awards including the 2012 R.W. Schwager Essay Prize, and the 2015 History Council SA Emerging Historian of the Year. She has won acclaim as a communicator of complex ideas to general audiences, and is a regular speaker at events, schools, community groups and in the media.

She hopes this book will satisfy all the people she meets at parties who want to know what Girardian theory is about, but don't really want her to give a lecture at the actual party.

Printed in the USA
CPSIA information can be obtained
at www.ICGtesting.com
CBHW080846220824
13508CB00023B/259

9 780646 960427